STUFF
DUTCH PEOPLE
BAKE

45 DELICIOUS RECIPES FOR CLASSIC DUTCH
COOKIES, PASTRIES, PIES & MORE!

Published in the Netherlands by Stuff Dutch People
Like

Some of the material in this book may have
originally appeared, in different form,
on the popular blog StuffDutchPeopleLike.com

Photo & other credits can be found on page 172

ISBN 978-90-828620-8-9

Printed in the EU

10 9 8 7 6 5 4 3 2 1

www.stuffdutchpeoplelike.com
www.facebook.com/stuffdutchpeoplelike
www.instagram.com/stuffdutchpeoplelike
www.twitter.com/stuffdutchlike

For media inquiries, corporate & volume sales or
any other request, please contact us at
hello@stuffdutchpeoplelike.com

CONTENTS

the Netherlands

DUTCH BAKING

For a relatively small country, the Dutch have an enormous history and repertoire of baked sweets and treats. Somewhat contradictory to their infamous Calvinistic roots, the Dutch have mastered the art of rich, indulgent baking. Many a joke has been made at the expense of modern-day Dutch cuisine (more mashed potatoes with kale, anyone?). However, we can not criticize their good sense of lavishly dunking a midday cookie into one's 4 o'clock coffee or their impressive spread of baked delights on special occasions.

When I first moved to the Netherlands, I instantly recognized quite a few Dutch baked goods. Not surprisingly, as I later found out that many Dutch recipes had also crossed the Atlantic. In fact, one of the very first Dutch cookbooks, *De Verstandige Kock (The Sensible Cook)*, published in 1667 and acknowledged as the definitive Dutch cookbook of the seventeenth century, was brought to North America by early Dutch settlers in the late 1600s. The pages of *The Sensible Cook* contain a litany of familiar baked goods — everything from tasty varieties of pancakes, pies, tarts and waffles to the precursors of the modern-day American gingerbread cookies (speculaas) and doughnuts (oliebollen).

In the Golden Age Netherlands, access to high quality baked goods was seen as a basic right, and not a luxury item reserved solely for the wealthy. The municipal governments regulated both the quality and price of items sold at local bakeries. This ensured that the price of a loaf of bread was set in accordance with the current price of grain — and not by that of an enterprising baker.

The Dutch have historically taken the art of baking very seriously. As early as the 17th century, governmental brood-wegers (bread inspectors) were appointed to ensure bakers met the correct requirements for the size, weight and quality of their bread. Complex guilds were set up for bakers, with the purpose of legitimizing the trade and ensuring the highest of quality. Guild members had to be official residents of the city and had to complete a certain number of training hours and pass several baking exams.

Special occasions in the Netherlands have always called for special food. Birthdays, Sinterklaas, New Year's Eve, King's Day and even the birth of a baby all have delectable desserts to call their own. Many of today's Dutch desserts and baked goods can be traced back to the pages of that very first cookbook. Of course modern variations exist and you won't find "cold rainwater" listed as an ingredient anymore, but you'd be surprised to read that the vast majority of recipes for Dutch baked goods haven't changed dramatically in the last four centuries.

THE BAKER BY JOB BERCKHEYDE (CA. 1681)

In this book we've tried to compile the most delicious examples of Dutch baking. Our first cookbook, *Stuff Dutch People Eat* was a surprise bestseller, both in the Netherlands and internationally. Since then we've been asked many times for more recipes — particularly for Dutch sweet treats. Whether you've been searching for the ideal appeltaart recipe like your Oma used to make or you would like to try your hand at a homemade ooey-gooey stroopwafel like the ones found on the streets of Amsterdam, this book is for you. We've searched high and low, tried and tested, and have found the best.

More importantly, you don't have to be Dutch to appreciate these recipes or the festive traditions that go along with them. I have grown accustomed to my (non-Dutch) husband making oliebollen no matter where in the world we are on New Year's Eve. ("Hello friends, don't mind my husband and the large vat of oil under his arm. I promise the mess will be worth it".) I've been known to enjoy kruidnoten all year round (tip: stock up on it in early December before it's all gone!) My Canadian-German children, born and raised here in Amsterdam, do in fact eat chocolate sprinkles on their bread for breakfast (don't judge me!). And I will admit that nothing beats a thick slice of ontbijtkoek with a decent helping of butter to start the day on a rainy grey morning.

I sincerely hope the recipes found in the pages of *Stuff Dutch People Bake* bring comfort, satisfaction and joy to your homes. Cooking and baking have become more a part of our lives this year than any of us could have imagined. Celebrations and entertaining in 2020 and beyond may look a little different, but the basics of any recipe will forever remain the same: mix ingredients with a healthy helping of love and you can never go wrong.

To my adopted country and its people: thank you for the inspiration — oh and the extra kilos! It was well worth every bite!

xo Colleen

October 2020

BREAKFAST
DELIGHTS

DUTCH BREAKFAST

The Dutch start their days in a relatively predictable fashion - as the standard Dutch breakfast is a rather simple affair. No elaborate cooking skills or time-consuming preparations are required. With a focus on practicality and ease, the Dutch breakfast, Monday through Friday, is most often a combination of two national staples: bread and dairy. Think a quick open-faced cheese or peanut-butter sandwich.

In this sense, Dutch breakfast and lunch do not differ greatly. Some bread "toppings" are primarily reserved for breakfast, including the beloved pindakaas (peanut butter), Nutella, appelstroop (a thick, sticky apple syrup), jam, and hagelslag. Hagel is the Dutch word for 'hail' and 'slag' literally translates to the words, 'strike or blow'. When combined they evoke the connotation of a hail storm.

Hagelslag is the Dutch answer to sprinkles and comes in several varieties (fruit-flavoured, white chocolate, milk chocolate, etc.). Dark chocolate remains the staple. Interestingly, the Dutch take their dark chocolate hagelslag categorisation very seriously. Only sprinkles with 32% cocoa or more can officially be called chocolade hagelslag. In most countries, sprinkles are primarily reserved for children, topping the likes of cakes and ice cream. In the Netherlands it is perfectly normal for Dutch adults to breakfast on thickly buttered slices of bread covered in chocolate sprinkles. Go figure!

There is, thankfully, a distinction between breakfast during the workweek and weekend, with the latter tending to be a wee bit more elaborate — but have no fear, the nation's Calvinistic roots don't allow for deliberate over indulgence.

In this chapter, you will find four popular Dutch breakfast recipes. Most are tasty weekend fare and are best paired with some form of thick stroop (syrup). If you really want to "double-down on your Dutchness," then go ahead and sprinkle a healthy dose of hagelslag on top! We won't tell anyone!

PANNENKOEKEN

Dutch pancakes

These delicious pannenkoeken are not just for pancake day! Larger and thinner than their American counterparts (yet thicker than crepes), Dutch pancakes are a popular dish in the Netherlands to be eaten as a main course, a dessert or a snack. Pannenkoeken are also very popular at children's birthday parties. They are most commonly eaten with syrup (stroop) or icing sugar. A tasty variation is appel-spekpannekoek which combines the saltiness of crispy bacon with the subtle sweetness of fresh apples for that perfectly sweet/savoury blend. The magic of pannenkoeken is that you can add whatever toppings you like, roll them up, and dive in!

⏱ 30 MIN   🍽 5 PANCAKES

INGREDIENTS

1 cup all-purpose flour

Pinch of salt

1 egg

1 cup milk

¼ tsp oil

INSTRUCTIONS:

1   In a large bowl, beat the egg until slightly foamy, then add the milk and salt. Mix in the flour slowly, whisking as you add, until the batter is smooth.

2   Heat a skillet over medium heat. Add a little butter to coat the skillet.

3   Add ½ cup of batter to the pan and swirl to coat the pan. Cook the pannenkoek over medium heat until it is just getting dry on the top and releases from the pan.

4   Flip the pannenkoek and cook on the other side until lightly golden.

5   Remove the pannenkoek from the pan and place on a platter.

TIP

Dutch people love drizzling copious amounts of suikerstroop on their pancakes. Looking for something more exotic? Add thin slices of apples and strips of fried bacon to the batter in the pan for the famous appel-spekpannekoek!

POFFERTJES
Dutch mini-pancakes

These fluffy little mini-pancakes are traditionally made from a mixture of wheat and buckwheat flour and are a very popular and delicious treat in the Netherlands. They can be found across the country at city markets, summer festivals, fairs and special Christmas markets. Poffertjes are made fresh and served with icing sugar, butter or syrup, and on occasion, whipped cream and strawberries. It's possible to find ready-made versions in supermarkets, but these lovely little guys aren't difficult to make and are definitely worth your while. The reward of making your own will be obvious after popping a warm poffertje into your mouth!

🕐 45 MIN   🍽 40-50 POFFERTJES

INGREDIENTS

½ cup warm milk

⅓ tsp active dry yeast

½ cup all-purpose flour

½ cup (light) buckwheat flour

1 egg

Pinch salt

Powdered sugar

Butter

INSTRUCTIONS:

1 Add yeast to warm milk and stir to combine. Allow to sit for about 10 minutes or until frothy.

2 When ready, mix the flour with the egg and slowly add the milk, beating well and making sure there are no lumps. Add in the pinch of salt.

3 Cover bowl with plastic wrap and let sit until bubbly and doubled in size, about 45 minutes.

4 Heat poffertjespan and lightly butter each dimple. Pour a small amount of batter into each dimple.

5 When small bubbles start to appear and the top starts to look a bit dried out, quickly flip poffertjes with a small fork. Allow poffertjes to cook on either side until nicely browned, then remove from pan.

6 Serve hot with a piece of butter and sprinkling of powdered sugar.

TIP
To make poffertjes you need a special poffertjespan!

WENTELTEEFJES

Dutch French toast

Wentelteefjes are very popular in the Netherlands and are the Dutch equivalent of French toast. A lovely blend of eggy, sugary, cinnamon sprinkled yumminess perfect for gracing any breakfast table, but also great for a light lunch as well. They are very easy and quick to make, and even better, wentelteefjes can be made with leftover or even slightly stale bread. Add strawberries for a little extra flavour, or even cheese, to make a perfect breakfast dish. The best thing about eating wentelteefjes is the contented faces of everyone at the table.

🕐 20 MIN　　🍽 8 SLICES

INGREDIENTS

8 slices of day-old bread

2 eggs

1 cup (¼ liter) lukewarm milk

¼ cup (60 grams) butter

2 tbsp sugar

1 tbsp cinnamon

Salt

INSTRUCTIONS:

1 Ideally use a larger, flat-bottomed bowl. Beat the eggs and stir in the milk, sugar, cinnamon and a pinch of salt.

2 Cut the crusts off the bread and fully soak the slices in the mixture. Butter a frying pan and fry the wentelteefjes on both sides until golden brown.

3 Serve hot with an extra sprinkle of sugar and cinnamon.

TIP
Tastes delicious with fresh fruit (e.g. strawberries, blueberries or bananas)

ONTBIJTKOEK

Dutch spiced cake

Ontbijtkoek, also known as "breakfast cake", is a spiced loaf generally made with rye, which gives it a lovely rich brown colour. It tastes even better eaten with a thick dollop of butter! Cinnamon, sugar and honey all feature in this popular breakfast cake. It's no wonder folks often grab a slice later in the day with a coffee. In the Netherlands, ontbijtkoek is often used as a party game for kids who try to take a bite out of the pieces of cake that are hung on strings above them! You can buy it in the supermarket, but it's never going to be quite as nice or as satisfying as when you make it yourself. So give it a try!

🕐 1 HOUR 10 MINS

🍽 1 LOAF

INGREDIENTS

1 cup rye flour

1 cup plain all purpose flour

3 tsp baking powder

2 tsp cinnamon

½ tsp each of ground cardamom, ginger, coriander seed and cloves

1 cup milk

½ cup brown sugar

½ cup honey

¼ cup molasses

¼ tsp salt

INSTRUCTIONS:

1 Preheat oven to 320°F (160°C) and grease a 20cm / 8 in cake tin.

2 Thoroughly mix all of the ingredients together in a mixing bowl. Pour the batter into the prepared tin and bake for ca. 60 - 80 minutes (test center with skewer after about 45 min).

3 Cool and serve in slices with lashings of butter.

BREAD
AND BUNS

BREAD

Bread has been a mainstay of the Dutch diet for centuries. Take a quick walk around Amsterdam's world-famous Rijksmusuem and you would be hard pressed to miss the hearty loaves of white, brown and multi-grain bread that appear in countless Golden Age paintings. In the seventeenth century, bread was a fixture of every daily meal; with cheese for breakfast, paired with meat or a hardy stew for midday, and combined with porridge in the evening.

The type of bread you ate in the Netherlands was also a symbol of status. Throughout the centuries, white bread was primarily reserved for the upper class — and mainly for special occasions. Luxuries such as suikerbrood (white bread baked with large clumps of sugar in the dough) were seen as quite an extravagance and often given to well-to-do families as a present after the successful birth of a baby. The Dutch working class ate rye bread, or coarse whole-wheat. A diet rich in carbohydrates and fats ensured that Dutch labourers, sailors, tradesmen and farmers slept with full bellies after long, hard work days. Of course, in these modern times, the notion of bread type and class is a thing of the past, but the Dutch's love of all-things-doughey has remained.

FUN FACTS:

The first weeks of marriage, the honeymoon period, are called in Dutch 'the white bread weeks' (wittebroodsweken). This is a reference to a 'luxury period' when the happy new couple was not to be disturbed.

The Dutch take their bread seriously: in the 17th century the government appointed broodwegers (bread inspectors) to ensure bakers met the correct requirements for the size and weight of their bread.

KRENTENBOLLEN
Dutch raisin buns

Dutch raisin buns: versatile and yummy. They are often made with a combination of raisins and currants. You can do a lot with these buns. You can even eat them plain thanks to those gooey little nuggets of fruit you hit every so often. They are perfect to eat warm, fresh out of the oven with melting butter or to pop in a lunch box for a tasty treat. In fact, they are very popular in the Netherlands as part of a school lunch and it's easy to see why kids love them. So go ahead and make a batch, you will thank us later!

3 HOURS   12 BUNS

INGREDIENTS

3 cups all-purpose flour

1 cup currants

1 cup dark raisins

2 tsp active dry yeast

1 cup warm milk

2 tbsp sugar

1 tsp salt

2 tbsp of soft, unsalted butter

1 large egg

½ tsp grated orange peel

½ tsp grated lemon peel

Line a large baking sheet with parchment paper

1 egg whisked (to glaze)

INSTRUCTIONS:

1. In a large bowl, mix the flour, salt, yeast and milk. Add egg, sugar, butter and citrus zests and stir thoroughly. Cover the bowl and let stand for 30 minutes.

2. Knead the mixture into a subtle dough (you can knead by hand or by machine). Then add the raisins and currants into the soft dough. Place the dough in a greased bowl, cover and let stand in a warm spot for 45 minutes.

3. Divide the dough into 12 equal portions and shape them into rolls, slightly flattened. Place on a baking sheet. Cover the rolls with a towel or oiled plastic wrap and allow them to rise until doubled, about 1 hour.

4. Preheat the oven to 400°F (200°C). Brush the rolls with the beaten egg and bake them for about 15-20 minutes until done. Enjoy with fresh butter. Yum!

MEERGRANENBROODJES
Multigrain rolls

Meergranenbroodjes are multigrain rolls and therefore especially healthy. They even use malt in place of sugar as a sweetener. These multigrain broodjes are the perfect base for any savoury sandwich and will be gobbled up at a weekend brunch. A generous helping of butter and a few slices of Dutch cheese and you have got yourself a perfect snack!

2 HOURS   8 BUNS

INGREDIENTS

2 tbsp barley malt syrup

1 ½ cups warm water

3 tsp active dry yeast

1 cup bread flour

1 cup whole wheat flour

1 cup rye flour

½ cup barley flour

2 tbsp sunflower seeds

2 tbsp flax seed

2 tbsp rolled oats

2 tsp salt

Topping

1 tbsp sunflower seeds

1 tbsp rolled oats

2 tbsp flax seed

INSTRUCTIONS:

1 Let barley malt syrup dissolve in the warm water and add the yeast. Let the mixture sit for about 5-10 minutes to let it proof. While you wait, whisk the various flours together and add the seeds and salt.

2 When the yeast is ready, stir it into the flour and mix until the dough comes together, then knead for a good 5-6 minutes. Shape the dough into a ball, leave it in a greased bowl, cover it and let it rest. Allow dough to rise at room temperature for around 40 minutes until it has doubled in size.

3 Roll the dough back into a ball. Sprinkle a bit of flour on the counter and relax the dough, covered, for about 10 minutes. In the meantime, put parchment paper on a baking sheet. Mix the seeds for the topping and place them in a bowl.

4 Slowly shape the dough into a circle, about seven inches wide. Use a sharp knife to split the dough into 8 wedges. Brush the top of each piece with a little bit of water, then dip the top into the seeds. Spread out the rolls on the baking sheet, with enough space to expand. Cover and let rise for about 30 minutes.

5 Heat the oven to 425°F (220°C) and bake the rolls for about 20 minutes. Enjoy with some extra butter and Dutch cheese!

VOLKORENBROOD
Whole-wheat bread

Bread plays an important role in the Netherlands and features in almost every meal. In many countries white bread and rolls are favoured, however the Dutch love their brown, whole-wheat bread variations. And whole-wheat bread is not only very tasty, but it's also full of fibre, vitamins and minerals. Nothing beats the aroma and taste of freshly baked bread.

⏱ 2 HOURS 30 MINS   🍽 1 LOAF OF BREAD

INGREDIENTS

4 cups whole-wheat flour

⅔ tbsp salt

1 cup cold tap water

1 ½ tbsp live yeast

2 tbsp olive oil

INSTRUCTIONS:

1. Dissolve the yeast in some of the water. Combine with flour, salt, water and start kneading the dough thoroughly. You can knead by hand or use a mixer with a dough hook attachment, adding up to ½ cup of additional water, as needed. After 15 minutes of kneading, you should have a wet and supple, but not sticky dough. When stretching the dough there shouldn't be any cracks.

2. Form the dough into a ball, wrap it in a warm and damp tea towel and allow it to rise for 30 to 45 minutes at room temperature. The dough should increase by about a third in volume. Remove the towel, smack the dough with your fists and then form it back into a ball. Wrap in the towel again and allow to rise for another 30 to 45 minutes.

3. Grease a bread tin with some olive oil.

4. Add some moisture to the work surface. Remove the towel from the dough and press the dough flat onto the work surface.

5. Shape the dough into a sausage-like shape with your hands, roughly the same length as the bread tin and place dough into the bread tin.

6. Cover the bread tin with the warm towel and allow the bread to rise for another 30 minutes (or until it has increased by a third in volume).

7. Preheat the oven to 428°F (220°C). Reduce the temperature to 392°F (220°C) and place the bread tin in the oven. Bake for 35 to 40 minutes.

8. If you knock on the baked bread, it should sound hollow. If it doesn't, return to the oven and bake a little longer. Remove the bread from the tin and allow it to cool.

TIP
Make sure to use freshly bought live yeast for best results!

PAASBROOD
Dutch Easter bread

Paasbrood is a traditional Easter bread filled with almond paste, golden raisins and candied lemon peel. It is part of the first day of an Easter feast in the Netherlands, celebrating the end of Lent as well as the coming of spring. Gatherings of friends and family to celebrate just wouldn't be the same without one of these loaves on the table. Most often it is made into a loaf, but it can also be made into rolls. It can be dusted with powdered sugar or even drizzled with a little icing for an extra treat.

🕐 2 HOURS 30 MINS   🍽 1 LOAF OF BREAD

INGREDIENTS

2 ½ cups flour

2 tsp salt

2 oz (50g) fresh yeast

1 cup milk, tepid

8 tbsp sugar

½ cup butter, melted

1 egg, whisked

Grated peel of 1 orange

10 oz (300g) currants, soaked, rinsed and dried

7 oz (200g) raisins, soaked, washed and dried

7 oz (200g) almond paste

Butter

Powdered sugar

INSTRUCTIONS:

1. Mix the yeast with some of the milk and create a paste.

2. In a separate bowl, mix flour, salt and sugar.

3. In another bowl, mix milk, egg and melted butter. This mixture should be lukewarm.

4. Make a hole in the flour mixture, pour in the wet ingredients and the yeast mixture and mix thoroughly.

5. Once properly mixed, knead it well by hand for 10 minutes. After kneading, the dough should be slightly sticky and smooth.

6. Mix in the grated orange peel, currants and raisins.

7. Place the dough in a bowl, cover with film and let rise in a warm spot for about 1 hour.

8. After letting the dough rise, knead it well and flatten the dough on a lined baking sheet to an oval 3 cm thick.

9. Shape the almond paste into a log, roughly 1 cm shorter than the dough shape. Now put the almond paste log on the dough and fold the sides of the dough over. Close well.

10. Cover with film and let the dough rise for another 30 minutes.

11. Brush the bread with milk and place in a preheated oven at 390°F (200°C).

12. Bake the paasbrood for about 40 minutes, cover it with foil when the fruits on the top get too dark. The bread is ready when it sounds hollow while tapping on the bottom.

13. Leave it to cool on a rack. Brush with butter and sprinkle with powdered sugar. Enjoy!

SÛKERBÔLE
Frisian sugar bread

Frisian suikerbrood (or Fryske Sûkerbôle in Frisian) is a Frisian luxury version of white bread containing large lumps of sugar mixed in with the dough. Suikerbrood is eaten throughout the Netherlands and Belgium, but as the name suggests is especially associated with the Dutch region of Friesland. Suikerbrood is usually flavored with cinnamon and ginger. Traditionally, this tasty bread was given as a present to mothers in Friesland who gave birth to a girl. The cinnamon and ginger were believed to have positive health effects. Most people nowadays eat suikerbrood for one reason only: it's so tasty!

🕐 2 HOURS 30 MINS   🍽 1 INCREDIBLE SUIKERBROOD

INGREDIENTS

4 cups flour

2 eggs

¾ stick of butter, melted

¾ cup warm milk

1 tsp dry active yeast

3 tbsp ginger syrup

1 tbsp ground cinnamon

½ cup crushed sugar cubes

Pinch of salt

INSTRUCTIONS:

1   In a small bowl whisk the yeast into the warm milk. In a separate large bowl, add the flour and salt and mix together. Now add the milk/yeast mixture and whisk together. Add the ginger syrup, eggs and ⅔ of the melted butter and knead together until you have a soft and flexible dough. Cover with a damp towel and let rise until the dough roughly doubleds in size.

2   Dust a counter with flour, roll out the dough and cover thoroughly with the sugar and cinnamon. Next, roll the suikerbrood dough into a loaf shape. Grease the inside of a bread pan with lots of butter. Add 1 tbsp of sugar to the pan and make sure the sugar coats the entire inside. Place the loaf inside and cover again for about 15 minutes.

3   Preheat the oven to 375°F (190°C). Brush the top of the loaf with the remaining butter. Then sprinkle the rest of the sugar on the top of the loaf. Place loaf in the oven and bake for about 30 minutes. Keep an eye on the suikerbrood to make sure the top doesn't brown too quickly.

4   Remove the suikerbrood and cool for about half an hour. Then try to gently loosen the bread from the bread pan. Be careful: suikerbrood is sticky!

KOEKJES

KOEKJES

Prior to living in the Netherlands, I had no idea that the beloved cookie — the backbone of any happy childhood — was a Dutch invention. It wasn't until I met an overzealous Dutch colleague, whose abundant nationalist pride had him convinced that every known item to man was created by the Dutch, that I learned of its true origins.

As my colleague Jaap* excitedly told me (and this time he was right), the word 'cookie' in American English first appeared in the early 19th century and is derived from the Dutch word 'koekje'. 'Koekje' is the diminutive version of the Dutch word for cake (koek), literally meaning 'little cake'.

Dutch cookies come in dozens of varieties in terms of shapes, ingredients and sizes, but they all have two things in common: 1) copious amounts of butter and 2) they are made to be dunked! Cookies in the Netherlands are not worthy unless they can be dipped into and served alongside a hot cup of coffee or tea.

FUN FACTS:

For the grammar geeks out there: the English spelling of Dutch words typically omitted combinations of vowels which do not exist in English (like "oe") and replaced them with existing vowel combinations respectively (like "oo"). Hence, the 'oe' in koekje became 'oo' in cookie.

Of course, legend goes that the Dutch are notoriously stingy and as an expat or tourist visiting the country you will be sure to hear the lore that locals will invite you over for coffee and then will proceed to quickly close the cookie tin, allowing guests to enjoy only one cookie per visit. I've heard this tale told over and over again but it certainly hasn't been my experience. Although with the addictive nature of Dutch cookies, it might actually be a good idea!

*when your memory fails you, change a Dutch person's name to Jaap, Joost or Jan.

STROOPWAFELS
Dutch syrup waffles

Stroopwafels are immensely popular crunchy wafer cookies sandwiched together with a deliciously sticky caramel filling. They were allegedly invented in the Dutch city of Gouda in the late 18th or early 19th century and are frequently sold fresh at markets and fairs. Stroopwafels are made by baking dough in a waffle maker, slicing the waffle in half and filling the insides with sweet caramel syrup. The only danger in making these cookies at home is that you may develop a serious stroopwafel addiction. Beware, there is no cure!

🕐 1 HOUR 30 MINS   🍽 12 WAFFLES

INGREDIENTS

For the dough:

4 cups all-purpose flour

½ tsp ground cinnamon

½ cup granulated sugar

1 cup unsalted butter

2 large eggs

1 package active dry yeast (¼ ounce)

½ cup warm water

For the filling:

1 ½ cups brown sugar

1 cup unsalted butter

1 tsp ground cinnamon

6 tbsp dark corn syrup

1 tbsp vanilla extract

INSTRUCTIONS:

1   In a mixer, add the flour, yeast, cinnamon and sugar and cut in the butter. Gradually pour in the warm water and let the dough mix thoroughly. Then add the eggs one at a time. Lastly add the pinch of salt and knead the dough well until it's nice and solid. Set aside to rise for 30 to 60 minutes.

2   In a saucepan melt the sugar and the butter, stirring slowly over a low heat. Add the cinnamon and the syrup and continue to stir until the filling slowly bubbles. Keep stirring to avoid burning! Ensure all the sugar has dissolved completely and the caramel filling is nice and creamy. Finally add the vanilla extract and mix it in. Keep the filling warm.

3   Roll dough into 12 small balls. Squeeze each ball into the preheated pizzelle iron or waffle maker and bake for about 30-40 seconds (check instructions). Once the waffle is baked you will have to move quickly (otherwise the waffle will be too hard to cut). Cut the waffle in half and cover the bottom half with a generous amount of filling. Place the top half back on top and press gently to ensure the filling spreads evenly. Set aside to cool.

TIP
Place a cold stroopwafel on a hot cup of coffee or tea and let it soften!

KLETSKOPPEN
Crunchy nut cookies

Is there anything better than a biscuit with your cup of tea or coffee? Especially if it's a really nice nutty, caramel biscuit that not only goes well with your chosen hot beverage, but could also be turned into a fabulous dessert with the addition of ice cream. Well, that is just what these lovely thin crunchy biscuits will do. Kletskoppen are traditional Dutch biscuits formerly known as kaalkoppen (baldheads) and can even be turned into a savoury snack by using hard cheese like parmesan. These wonderful crispy sweet biscuits full of peanuts or almonds are a truly diverse treat and make a delicate and tasty snack.

 30 MIN   ▯◎▯ 20 COOKIES

INGREDIENTS

4 tbsp butter, room temperature

½ tsp cinnamon

¼ cup peanuts

½ cup brown sugar, tightly packed

⅓ cup flour

INSTRUCTIONS:

1 Mix butter with the sugar and cinnamon and add flour slowly until absorbed, then mix in the peanuts.

2 Preheat the oven to 400°F (200°C).

3 The dough should be slightly sticky and workable. If it's too sticky just add a bit of flour, then try again.

4 Line your baking sheet with a double lining of parchment paper. Roll the dough into tiny marbles, spread them evenly and then flatten each one thoroughly with the palm of your hand.

5 Bake for about 5 minutes. The dough can burn quickly so make sure to keep an eye on it! Enjoy!

TIP
Kletskoppen can also be added to other desserts as an extra garnish (e.g. ice cream).

BOKKENPOOTJES

Almond meringue cookies

Bokkenpootjes can be literally translated from Dutch as "goats' feet". They are rolled into logs and dipped in chocolate on both ends, somewhat resembling the feet of goats! This doesn't sound very appetising, but trust me they really are. These cookies are in fact splendid and made with almond meringue and dipped in dark chocolate. The filling between these cookies is either made with a light white chocolate and vanilla blend or with butter cream, which makes these lovely little cookies even more tempting as a sweet treat, especially with a coffee.

🕒 30 MIN   🍽 20 COOKIES

INGREDIENTS

8 egg whites

1 ¾ cups white sugar

5 ¼ cups almond meal

1 tsp ground cinnamon

Zest from 1 lemon

1 tsp vanilla extract

For the filling:

3 ½ tbsp butter

1 ¼ cups confectioners' sugar, sifted

¼ tsp vanilla extract

4 oz (120g) bittersweet chocolate, chopped

INSTRUCTIONS:

1. Beat egg whites until frothy in a large mixing bowl. Slowly add the sugar and continue to beat until stiff. Mix in the almond meal, lemon zest, cinnamon and vanilla.

2. Line a baking sheet with parchment paper and transfer the mixture (meringue) to a piping bag or similar. Squeeze the meringue into ladyfingers about 3 inches (8 cm) long. Let the unbaked cookies dry at room temperature for about 2 hours.

3. Preheat an oven to 320°F (160°C).

4. Bake the cookies until dried but not yet brown for about 15 to 20 minutes. Allow them to cool completely.

5. Make the cookie filling by mixing the butter and confectioners' sugar until smooth. Mix in the vanilla. In the meantime, melt the chocolate.

6. Assemble the cookies by spreading the cream filling on the back of a cookie, place it on top of another cookie, and finally dip both ends in the melted chocolate. Leave the bokkenpootjes to dry on waxed paper or parchment.

GEVULDE KOEK
Marzipan stuffed cookie

These are one of the most popular sweet cookies found in bakeries and markets throughout the Netherlands. In almost every train station you will find a kiosk selling these cookies. If you are in a hurry, no worries, you can almost always count on being able to purchase one on the train. What a great way to travel, enjoying a gevulde koek and a hot drink! Gevulde koeken are made with a buttery dough filled with a sweet almond paste. The cookies are dome-shaped, have shiny tops and often have an almond or three placed on top as decoration. There's no need to catch a train though, you can make these at home, grab a hot drink and enjoy a well-deserved break.

L 30 MIN   8 COOKIES

INGREDIENTS

For the dough:

2 ¼ cups all-purpose flour

½ cup sugar

1 tsp baking powder

Pinch of salt

1 tbsp cold water

1 ¾ sticks butter

For the filling:

1 cup almond paste

2 tbsp sugar

1 egg white

2 tbsp water

1 tsp almond extract

For brushing:

1 egg yolk

1 tbsp milk

8 sliced or whole almonds

INSTRUCTIONS:

1   Mix the butter and dry ingredients into a dough. Add 1 tbsp cold water and knead the dough until all the butter is well mixed. Form into an oval shape, cover with film and place in the fridge.

2   To make the filling, crumble the almond paste and beat it thoroughly with the rest of the ingredients until it's foamy. If it's a bit too runny, add a tablespoon of flour.

3   Preheat your oven to 350°F (180°C). Take the dough out of the fridge and cut it in half. Roll one half out, to about ⅛ of an inch thick. Cut out 8 circles. Roll the other half out and cut another 8 circles. Place one large teaspoon of almond paste mix in the middle of a circle and carefully add a second circle on top. Then seal the edges with a fork.

4   Place the unbaked koeken on a parchment lined baking sheet. Beat the egg yolk with the milk and brush the top of the koeken, then place an almond on top. Bake for about 15 minutes or until golden.

KRAKELINGEN
Sweet Dutch pretzels

Krakelingen look a lot like pretzels, but while pretzels are known for being salty, savoury snacks, krakelingen are sweet. Most krakelingen found in bakeries in the Netherlands now are mechanically made; however, there are still a few bakeries where the traditional yeast dough is rolled by hand. They can be either crispy or soft, depending on which you prefer. The smaller you make them, the crispier they are. If you do bake some krakelingen, be careful, the divine smell might even have your neighbors knocking at your door!

L **2 HOURS 30 MINS**   **8 SERVINGS**

INGREDIENTS

1 cup all-purpose flour

1 ½ tsp instant yeast

2 tbsp granulated sugar

¼ tsp salt

3 ⅓ tbsp tepid milk

½ cup butter (melted)

1 egg (loosely beaten)

1 cup pure cane
or brown sugar

INSTRUCTIONS:

1 Add the flour, granulated sugar, yeast and salt in a large bowl. Add the butter, milk and egg and mix the wet and dry ingredients together thoroughly. Place dough on a floured surface and knead until it forms a soft, non-sticky dough.

2 Shape the dough into a ball and place it back into the bowl. Cover the bowl with plastic film (or a damp towel) and put it in a warm place. Wait until the dough has almost doubled in volume.

3 Sprinkle a third of the brown sugar over a baking sheet and pour the rest into a large plate.

4 Punch the dough down with your fist and knead it thoroughly until smooth again. Divide the dough into 16 equal pieces and spread out on the baking sheet, ensuring that each piece is evenly coated with sugar. Then set the sugared dough portions to one side.

5 Take a portion of sugared dough and roll it back and forth on a clean surface creating a long and thin tube shape of about 12 inches (30 cm). Roll the tube through the sugar on the plate, ensuring it is thoroughly covered, fold in half and then roll the tube back and forth until it measures about the same length as before.

6 Place the tube in the sugar on the baking sheet and set aside. Do the same with the remaining pieces of dough.

7 Add parchment paper to a baking sheet. Twist the tubes into small pretzel shapes and place the pretzels on the baking sheet. Cover the baking sheet with plastic film and allow to rise in a warm place. The pretzels should roughly double in size.

8 Preheat the oven to 390°F (200° C). Bake the krakelingen for about 10 to 15 minutes until golden brown, but make sure to keep an eye on them. They burn quickly once the sugar starts to caramelize.

9 Remove the krakelingen from the oven and allow them to cool.

EIERKOEKEN
Dutch egg cakes

Eierkoeken are delicious golden yellow egg cakes. They are versatile and flat bottomed with a domed top and can be eaten plain or with butter. They can be topped with icing sugar or even sandwiched together with cream and topped with fruit. These soft delights can be used for everything from a snack to a dessert, depending on what you add to them. In 2006, the sale of eierkoeken increased tenfold in the Netherlands! Why, you ask? "Diet guru" and celebrity Sonja Bakker started recommending these egg cakes as a "responsible snack". Well, we won't claim that they help you lose weight, but they sure make for a delicious and light-ish snack!

🕐 30 MIN   🍽 20 COOKIES

INGREDIENTS

4 eggs

¾ cup sugar

1 ¼ cups flour

1 tbsp + 1 tsp baking powder

INSTRUCTIONS:

1 Preheat the oven to 360°F (180°C).

2 Line two baking sheets with parchment paper. Take a large bowl and whisk the eggs and sugar for about 2-3 minutes until foamy. Slowly add the flour and baking powder and mix thoroughly.

3 Use a large spoon to place six large scoops of batter on each baking sheet. Make sure to leave enough room between the dough.

4 Place one rack at the time into the oven.

5 Bake the eierkoeken for 10-15 minutes until golden brown. Don't bake them too long; they should remain nice and soft.

6 Allow the eierkoeken to cool.

TIP
In the Dutch province of Brabant they like to spread butter on their eierkoeken and sprinkle them with sugar. Give it a try!

BITTERKOEKJES

Dutch almond macaroons

Bitterkoekjes are Dutch macaroons, made with bitter almonds, sugar and eggs. Ground hazelnuts can also be substituted for the bitter almonds. They are similar to Italian amaretti cookies but with a chewy rather than a crunchy centre. While they can be made and eaten at any time of the year, they are very popular at Christmas as the almond taste makes a perfect match for a cup of hot cocoa. They are also delicious served with coffee and ice cream. Bitterkoekjes can be a bit tricky to master, but once you've got the hang of it, you'll never buy store-bought versions again!

🕐 30 MIN   🍽 CA. 25 BITTERKOEKJES

INGREDIENTS

3 cups almond meal

1 ½ cups sugar

4 tsp almond essence

4 egg whites

INSTRUCTIONS:

1 Preheat the oven to 350°F (185°C).

2 Mix the almond meal, sugar and almond essence in a large bowl.

3 Slowly add in the egg whites and mix thoroughly to a solid dough.

4 Place baking paper on a baking sheet and add small amounts of batter (size of a teaspoon) spread out over the baking paper (press down gently with a damp finger).

5 Bake the bitterkoekjes until golden brown for approx. 10-15 minutes.

KERSTKRANSJES
Dutch Christmas cookies

Christmas is full of delicious treats that make the festive season even more special. This is true of kerstkransjes, or little Christmas wreaths, that gain their name from their wreath shape. These yummy little cookies appear around the festive season and were traditionally hung on the Christmas tree. They can be decorated with sugar strands, almonds, chocolate or even icing. They all have one thing in common: the hole used to hang them up! What's brilliant about these cookies is that they are simple to make and can be a great family activity with kids on cold, rainy or snowy days!

🕐 30 MIN   25 KERSTKRANSJES

INGREDIENTS

2 cups all-purpose flour

1 pinch salt

⅓ cup sugar

2 tbsp vanilla sugar (or 1 tsp vanilla extract)

lemon zest of half a lemon

¼ tsp almond essence

1 egg

½ stick cold butter

Topping

1 egg lightly beaten

3 tbsp coarse sugar

3 tbsp thinly sliced almonds

INSTRUCTIONS:

1 Add the first 8 ingredients into a bowl.

2 With the help of two butter knives, cut the butter and mix thoroughly with all the ingredients until it resembles a crumbly texture.

3 Use your hands to shape the cookie dough into a ball and wrap in plastic wrap. Place in the fridge to chill for 15 minutes.

4 In the meantime, preheat the oven to 350°F (175°C) and line a baking tray with parchment paper.

5 Flour a work surface and roll out the dough, roughly 1.7 inch (4cm) thick. With a round, ideally scallop-edged cookie cutter, cut out the cookies. With a smaller, round cookie cutter, cut a hole in the middle of the cookie. Spread the cut-out cookies on the baking tray.

6 Lightly beat an egg and brush every cookie evenly with some of the egg. Sprinkle coarse sugar and thinly sliced almonds on top of the cookies.

7 Bake the kerstkransjes for about 15 minutes or until golden.

CAKES
AND TAARTEN

CAKES AND TAARTEN

The Dutch are known for their unique take on cakes, flans and pies — which they have been making for centuries. We've all heard the common expression in English "It's as American as apple pie", but it turns out apple pie isn't actually American after all! This tasty dessert is in fact yet another item that early Dutch (and in this case, also British) settlers brought over to America in the 1600s — along with the apples themselves! There is nothing more Dutch then sitting in a cozy cafe and ordering an appeltaart met slagroom (Dutch apple pie with whipped cream). This delectable pie will satisfy, sustain and delight!

Different regions of the Netherlands also gave their name to different Dutch desserts. Take for instance, the famous Limburgse vlaai (Limburg flan/pie), which is a pie or tart consisting of a pastry and filling. This pie is historically associated with the provinces of Limburg found in the Netherlands, Belgium, as well as Germany.

In the Netherlands vlaai is eaten on special occasions and significant life events, such as birthdays and funerals (when the vlaai is typically made with black plum). It's customary to bring cake to work for all your colleagues to enjoy on your birthday, a tradition I admit that I had a hard time getting used to ("What? I have to be the one to bake my own birthday cake? And every year!"). Thankfully, in today's busy modern world Dutch pie shops can be found conveniently in every neighbourhood, catering to the "bring your own cake to work" crowd!

APPELTAART

Dutch apple pie

Appeltaart is Dutch apple pie and really, is there anything nicer than a warm apple pie? It can be eaten plain, but the addition of whipped cream or ice cream makes it even nicer! You can buy a slice of delicious appeltaart at almost any cafe in the Netherlands. The traditional appeltaart has been around since the Middle Ages, and no wonder, since most people find it irresistible. The Dutch version of apple pie contains just a few simple ingredients and is usually much deeper than its American or English counterparts (at least 2" deep) and decorated with a beautiful lattice top.

🕐 2 HOURS 15 MINS   🍽 1 LEKKER APPELTAART

INGREDIENTS

11 oz (300 g) self-rising flour

7 oz (200 g) butter

5 oz (150 g) light brown sugar

¾ egg for the dough

¼ beaten egg for brushing

Pinch of salt

2 lb (1 kg) apples

Fresh lemon juice

2 tsp ground cinnamon

¼ cup (50 g) sugar

⅓ cup (50 g) dry raisins (optional)

INSTRUCTIONS:

1   Mix flour, salt, brown sugar and butter in cubes. Add the ¾ egg and nicely knead the ingredients into a smooth dough. Leave to rest in the fridge for an hour.

2   Peel the apples and cut into thick slices. Add the slices into a separate bowl and sprinkle with lemon juice, cinnamon and sugar and stir. Add the raisins (optional). Cover and set aside.

3   Preheat the oven to 350°F (175°C). Line a round buttered baking tin (20-22 cm) with two-thirds of the dough. Add the prepared apples and distribute the slices evenly.

4   With the remaining dough make a grid on top of the apples. In a small bowl add the ¼ egg and a bit of water and stir. Brush the grid lightly with the egg mixture.

5   Bake the appeltaart for about 60 - 70 minutes.

TIP
Serve warm or cold with whipped cream or a scoop of vanilla ice cream!

KERSENVLAAI

Dutch cherry pie

Sweet cherry pie! Cherries are a wonderful fruit and can be found in abundance in the Netherlands, but only for a short time each year, which is why so many people pick and preserve them. This scrumptious pie can be made with real cherries, but out of season you can take full advantage of preserved or canned cherries. Often made in winter, this pie is a perfect taste of summer in the cold months. Warm and so sweet from the oven, it's a pie lover's dream!

 2 HOURS 🍽 1 YUMMY KERSENVLAAI

INGREDIENTS

For the dough:

2 cups (300g) all-purpose flour

3 tbsp sugar

1 egg yolk

⅔ cup (150ml) slightly warm milk

2 tbsp (25g) butter

20g fresh yeast, or 3g active dry yeast

pinch of salt

For the filling:

1.5 lb (700g) cherries in syrup

2 tbsp sugar

2 tbsp cornstarch

For the glaze:

1 egg yolk

1 tbsp milk

1 tbsp sugar

9/10 in (24 cm) vlaai mold or similar tart pan

INSTRUCTIONS:

1 Dissolve the yeast and sugar in milk and let stand for 10-15 minutes.

2 In a large bowl, add flour, salt and sugar and combine. Add milk and egg and mix. Finally add the soft butter.

3 Knead for 5-10 minutes with an electric mixer or for 10-15 minutes by hand. The dough should be smooth and elastic. Put the dough in a greased bowl, cover and let it rest for 1-1.5 hours in a warm place (the dough should roughly double in volume).

4 For the filling, drain the cherries and put the syrup in a saucepan over medium heat. In a small bowl, combine 4 tbsp syrup with cornstarch and whisk well until completely dissolved. Pour the cornstarch mixture and sugar into the hot cherry syrup and mix well. Cook over low heat and stir frequently until the mixture is nice and thick. Remove from the heat and add cherries. Set aside and let cool completely.

5 Preheat the oven to 430°F (220°C). Prepare a 9/10 inch (24cm) vlaai mold or similar tart pan by greasing it with butter or spraying it with some oil. Take about ⅔ of the dough and roll it into a nice circle, about 0.12 inch (3mm) thick. Leave the excess dough hanging over the edges, but make sure the dough inside the mold is neatly fitted. Cover it and let it sit for about 10 minutes.

6 Now with a rolling pin, trim off the edges / excess dough by carefully pressing it along the rim of the mold. Add the cherry pie filling and distribute evenly. Roll out the remaining dough and cut it into strips of about 0.5 inches (1.5 cm) wide. Place the strips over the filling to create a criss-cross lattice pattern.

7 Brush the lattice with egg wash (a yolk lightly beaten with 1 tablespoon of milk) and sprinkle with brown sugar. Put the vlaai in the oven and bake for about 25-30 minutes.

8 Remove from the oven, place on a wire rack and leave to cool for 20 minutes, then remove the pie from the tin and let it cool completely. Serve with a dollop of whipped cream!

RIJSTEVLAAI

Dutch rice pudding pie

This pie's filling is a variety of creamy rice pudding and is one of the most popular Dutch pies. It is traditionally served cold, perhaps with whipped cream on the side. They are easy to bake, and a hit with young and old. While it is called a pie, it is really more of a flan, having no crust on top. Vlaai in general is eaten on special occasions: birthdays, family parties, get togethers, and even funerals in the Netherlands, especially in the province of Limburg.

🕑 **2 HOURS 30 MINS** 🍽 **1 DELICIOUS RIJSTEVLAAI**

INGREDIENTS

For the filling

½ cup short grain rice

⅓ cup sugar

4 cups whole milk

2 tbsp of sugar

2 tsp vanilla essence

2 eggs, divided

Pinch of salt

For the dough

1 tbsp sugar

2 tbsp butter

1 ¾ cups flour

½ cup milk, warm

1 egg, beaten

2 tsp active dry yeast

INSTRUCTIONS:

1 Thoroughly wash and rinse the rice. Boil the milk, then add the rice, salt and sugar. Cover and simmer on low for 1 hour. Finally add the vanilla, stir well and set aside to cool.

2 Add the yeast in the warm milk and let it proof. In a large mixing bowl add the flour and then the yeast mixture. Whisk in the sugar, butter and egg, and knead into a soft yet solid dough. Cover and set aside in a warm place to rise.

3 Whisk the egg yolks with the two tablespoons of sugar until creamy. Separately beat the egg whites until stiff. Add the egg yolks to the rice, mix thoroughly and then fold in the stiff egg whites.

4 Grease a pie dish (11 inches) or metal pan. Punch down the dough, roll it out and line the pie pan. Using a fork, poke holes all over the surface, then cover and let the dough rise again.

5 Preheat oven to 390°F (200°C). Evenly pour the rice filling into the pie dish and bake for approximately 40 minutes (if the top browns too quickly, cover with some aluminum foil). Let the pie cool in the pan for about 30 minutes, then remove and leave to cool on a rack. The rice filling will set as it cools.

TIP
Rijstevlaai is best served cold. And it's one of those pies that tastes even better the next day!

KRUIMELVLAAI
Dutch crumb pudding pie

The Dutch crumb pie, or kruimelvlaai, is a sweet vanilla pudding topped with golden crumbs. It's perfect with your afternoon coffee or any time of day. This vlaai has a delightful soft base filled with creamy vanilla and a crunchy top, lightly dusted with powdered sugar. Sweet, simple and delicious, it's definitely one to make at home. And it's sure to be a big hit with family and friends!

L 2 HOURS   1 LEKKER KRUIMELVLAAI

INGREDIENTS

For the dough

1 ½ cups flour

½ stick butter, room temperature

⅓ cup warm milk

1 small egg

½ tsp of active dry yeast

1 tbsp sugar

1 tsp salt

For the filling

2 cups store-bought vanilla pudding

For the streusel

1 cup flour

1 stick butter

½ cup sugar

INSTRUCTIONS:

1   Mix the yeast into the warm milk and set it aside to proof. Whisk together the flour with the sugar and salt. Once the yeast has proofed, add it to the flour and mix well for a minute. Now add the egg and continue to mix. Once the dough starts coming together, add in the butter. Knead everything thoroughly until you have a dough that's not too sticky but also not too dry. Place the dough in a greased bowl, cover with a damp cloth and let it rise.

2   For the kruimel, cut the butter into the flour and sugar until it feels like wet sand.

3   Butter a 9 inch x 1.25 pie form and line the form with the dough. Using a fork, poke holes in the dough, cover and leave to rise again until puffy.

4   Preheat oven to 400°F (200°C). Pour the cooled vanilla pudding into the pie form (on top of the dough) and cover thoroughly with the kruimel. Bake for about 15-20 minutes.

BOTERKOEK

Dutch butter cake

Boterkoek translates to "butter cake" and that's just what it is, a deeply dense deliciously buttery cake made with only a few ingredients. Little wonder that it's usually eaten in smaller slices. A small piece of this rich cake will please everyone's sweet tooth. This indulgent moist treat works wonderfully with a coffee, tea, or hot chocolate. It is truly the perfect comfort food to share with friends.

🕐 1 HOUR   🍽 1 BUTTERY BOTERKOEK

INGREDIENTS

1 cup butter (cold)

1 cup sugar (fine)

1 tbsp vanilla sugar or 1 tsp vanilla extract

1 tsp lemon zest

Pinch of salt

2 eggs

2 cups flour

INSTRUCTIONS:

1 Mix the flour with the sugar, salt, one egg, vanilla and lemon zest. Cut in the butter and knead the dough until it all comes together

2 Once the dough is formed, take it out of the bowl and if needed, lightly knead it on a floured surface.

   Flatten the dough and wrap it in cling film. Leave the dough in the fridge to cool for at least 30 minutes.

3 Preheat the oven to 350°F (175°C). Grease a butter cake pan and press the dough into the cake pan.

4 Using a fork, make markings on the dough to create a pattern. Beat the second egg and thoroughly brush the top of the butter cake.

5 Bake in the oven for 20-25 minutes until golden. Set aside to cool completely.

TIP
Boterkoek is often served in small triangular slices or little cubes

SPEKKOEK
Indonesian layer cake

Spekkoek or 'bacon cake' evolved during colonial times in the Dutch East Indies and is a blend of Dutch and Indonesian cooking. It is thought the cake was served for evening tea by the wives of Dutch administrators in Batavia (Jakarta). There is no actual bacon in this cake, but the name literally translates to pork belly, due to its multilayer look. The layers of spekkoek are usually flavoured with spices such as cloves, cinnamon, cardamom, ginger and nutmeg. Each layer is carefully prepared and baked separately. It may be a complex cake to bake, but the spectacular results will be well worth it!

🕐 1 HOUR 15 MIN    1 MAGNIFICENT SPEKKOEK

INGREDIENTS

1 cup flour

1 cup butter, softened

1 cup sugar

10 large eggs, separated

Pinch of salt

2 tsp cinnamon

1 tsp ginger

½ tsp nutmeg

½ tsp cardamom

¼ tsp clove

INSTRUCTIONS:

1. In a large bowl, cream butter and sugar together with an electric mixer. Then whisk in the egg yolks. In another bowl, beat egg whites with salt until stiff and mix into the yolk mixture. Then mix in the flour.

2. Divide batter into two bowls. Add the spices to one bowl and stir well.

3. Line the bottom of a buttered 9 inch (23 cm) round cake pan with wax paper and grease the wax paper with butter. Pour about ½ cup of the spice batter into the pan, forming a thin layer.

4. Place the pan under a preheated broiler for 2 minutes, or until the layer is firm and very lightly browned (don't leave it unattended). Spread ½ cup of the plain batter over the top, spread into a thin layer and broil until firm. Repeat layering and broiling until all batter is used. Let cake cool, then remove from pan.

TURKEY PIE BY PIETER CLAESZ (1627)

TABLE WITH ORANGE, OLIVES AND PIE BY CLARA PEETERS (1611)

DUTCH
PASTRIES

KING'S DAY

King's Day (formerly known as Queen's Day) is one of the most revered Dutch national holidays. Now celebrated on April 27th, the date commemorates the birth of the current King Willem-Alexander. The first Queen's Day was celebrated in 1885 for Queen Whilhelmina, the current King's great-grandmother.

For a nation which often insists on "acting normal" (doe maar gewoon), the collective behaviour of the Dutch on King's Day is truly nothing of the sort. April 27th seems to be the one day of the year when the Dutch break all their self-imposed rules and let loose in a way that puts all other nations to shame. To say that King's Day is the world's greatest party is nothing short of an understatement. Put concisely as possible: **LONG LIVE THE KING!!**

Orange is the national colour of the Netherlands and in celebration of *Koningsdag*, the entire country dresses in orange. The cities celebrate in true Dutch fashion, with a sort of 'anything goes' tolerance. With street parties, live music, boat parades and citizens allowed to sell anything anywhere (including food, non-alcoholic drinks and baked goods!), Dutch cities and towns burst with colourful revelry. It's a great time to grab a bargain or earn yourself some extra cash.

If you haven't experienced the pure joviality and joy of a city flooded in *oranje*, I dare say you haven't truly lived. Bells sound, bands play, children perform, deals are made, bargains are snatched, drinks are consumed, and above all, love, laughter and smiles abound.

For a nation often divided, King's Day is the great equalizer. Unlike other countries' national days, April 27th is not about in-your-face patriotism or royal worshiping, it's about oneness. Everyone can participate, everyone can partake, everyone can carve out their own way to celebrate and anyone can do so with the simple act of throwing on an orange t-shirt and joining the *gezellige* crowds.

TOMPOUCE
Dutch mille-feuille

Tompouces are lovely treats consisting of two layers of puff pastry generously filled with a sweet pastry cream. They are very similar to the French mille-feuille, but with much more custard filling. The top layer usually has a covering of smooth pink icing which is changed to orange icing on King's Day to honour the royal family. Since 1990, the tompouce also has orange icing when the Dutch football team plays at international football tournaments. They are frequently served as part of afternoon tea or on special occasions. These flaky, creamy delights are not easy to eat without getting a little messy, but it's well worth it!

 45 MINS   8

INGREDIENTS

For the pastry:
Ready-rolled puff pastry

1 egg whites beaten

For the custard:
1 cup whole or skim milk

1 tsp vanilla extract

Pinch of salt

2 eggs yolks

$\frac{1}{5}$ cup (40 g) granulated sugar

Zest of 1 lemon

2 tbsp corn flour

For the glaze:
1 cup (100 g) powdered sugar

1 egg, whites only, beaten

1 lemon, zest and $\frac{1}{2}$ teaspoon of the juice

INSTRUCTIONS:

1 Preheat the oven to 400°F (205 °C). Spray a baking sheet with cooking spray. Cut the puff pastry into rectangular pieces (typical tompouce are ca. 2.5 inches x 5 inches or 6 cm x 12 cm). Place pastry rectangles on the baking sheet and brush with egg. Bake for 10-15 minutes or until the pastry turns golden brown.

2 In a bowl beat the egg yolks, then add sugar and the lemon zest and whisk until light and foamy. Add the corn flour and a few tablespoons of warm milk and whisk to prevent lumps.

3 In a saucepan heat the milk with the vanilla and salt over a low heat. Add the egg mixture and whisk continuously until the custard is nice and thick. Remove from the heat and press some plastic wrap onto the surface of the custard to prevent a skin from forming.

4 Combine the powdered sugar, lemon juice, egg white and zest to create the glaze. Whisk for about five minutes.

5 Hold the hot pastry in a kitchen towel and carefully slice each rectangle into 2 layers with a sharp knife (be careful not to burn yourself!). Take the bottom part of a baked pastry and spread the cooled custard on it. Place the other pastry half on top and glaze thoroughly.

ROZE KOEK
Dutch pink cakes

Roze koek, or 'pink cake' is actually a large Dutch cup cake topped with a layer of silky, very pink icing. They are quite simple to make, but that bright pink icing makes them stand out from the crowd. A true favourite, these simple yummy treats will be ones you come back to again and again. The cake itself has the usual familiar ingredients: sugar, eggs, butter and flour, but that pink icing makes all the difference, turning it into something special. Roze koeken are those cakes that bring back nostalgic childhood memories!

⏱ 2 HOURS 15 MINS   🍽 4-6 SERVINGS

INGREDIENTS

2 sticks butter, room temperature

1 ½ cups sugar

1 tsp lemon zest

4 eggs

1 ¾ cups flour

For the icing

6 heaping tbsp powdered sugar

2 tbsp red raspberry juice

Red food coloring (optional)

Milk (optional)

INSTRUCTIONS:

1 In a bowl, mix the butter with the sugar. Gradually add eggs and beat until fully absorbed before adding the next one. Lastly, slowly add the lemon zest and the flour into the mix until you have a pourable thick batter.

2 Preheat oven to 390°F (200°C). Grease a muffin pan fill each cup half full of batter. With a (wet) spoon flatten the top. Bake dough for about 20 minutes until golden.

3 Let muffins cool on a wire rack. Cut off the tops of the muffins (if necessary) to have a nice flat surface.

4 Mix the powdered sugar with the berry juice and stir well. Add some milk if it gets too thick (if you want a strong pink colouring, you may have to add a drop of red food coloring). Ice the cakes with the pink coating. Let the icing dry, then serve with coffee or tea.

BOSSCHE BOLLEN
Dutch cream puff

Bossche bol or 'chocolate ball' is a very large cream puff ball that originated from the Dutch city of Den Bosch. They are like giant profiteroles, a pastry ball filled with whipped cream and completely covered with dark chocolate. Yum! They can be messy to eat. Dutch traditionalists don't use a fork, instead they hold them upside down so the whipped cream won't drip out. What's a little mess if it means you get to eat one of these delectable chocolate bollen with your afternoon coffee!

🕐 1 HOUR 30 MIN   🍽️ 4 BOSSCHE BOLLEN

INGREDIENTS

⅓ cup flour

⅓ cup water

2 tbsp butter

1 egg, beaten

Pinch of salt

½ cup semi-sweet chocolate chips

1 tbsp water

½ cup whipping cream

2 tbsp sugar

INSTRUCTIONS:

1   Add the water and butter to a saucepan over medium heat. Take off the stove as soon as it boils. Whisk in the flour and stir thoroughly until the batter comes together in a ball. Add the pinch of salt, mix in the egg and continue to stir until the batter is a homogenous dough.

2   Preheat oven to 375°F (190°C). Place parchment paper on a baking sheet, divide the dough in two or four balls and place them on top of the parchment. Bake for about 20-25 minutes or until puffy and golden. Remove and let cool.

3   Beat the whipping cream and sugar until stiff. Take a pastry bag with a small tip and poke through the bottom of the bol. Fill the dough balls with whipped cream.

4   Melt the chocolate chips and tablespoon of water in the microwave (30 seconds on medium). Stir until the chocolate has melted completely. Leave to cool for about 10 minutes, then carefully dip the cream-filled dough balls, head first, into the chocolate.

5   Cool the Bossche bollen in the fridge for about 20 minutes or until the chocolate has solidified.

APPELFLAP
Dutch apple turnovers

Appelflappen (or Dutch apple turnovers) are fruit-filled parcels of yumminess. Appelflappen are one of the most well known and well loved Dutch pastry treats. A triangular pocket of puff pastry filled with sweetened apples, raisins/currants, cinnamon and sometimes apricots. The top layer of pastry is additionally covered in granular sugar. Appelflappen are a perfect treat to pair with a hot drink, especially in the autumn when apples are in abundance!

🕒 45 MINS   8 APPELFLAPPEN

INGREDIENTS

2 tbsp currants

2 tbsp raisins

½ cup apple juice

3 dried apricots

2 apples

2 tbsp sugar

Pinch of cinnamon

1 lb (450g) puff pastry

Coarse sugar

INSTRUCTIONS:

1   In a bowl, mix the currants with the raisins and apple juice. Add the dried apricots to a small cup and add enough warm water to cover. Ideally soak the currants, raisins and apricots overnight (or at least for a few hours).

2   Peel and core the apples, then chop into small pieces. Drain and then add the raisins and currants to the apples and stir well. Mince the apricots until almost a pulp and then fold them into the apple mixture. Finally add the sugar and cinnamon and mix well.

3   Unfold the puff pastry and cut into squares, 4.5 x 4.5 in (11.5 x 11.5 cm) approximately. Add about ¼ cup of filling onto the bottom half of the square, wet the edges of the dough and then fold the top part over, creating a triangle. Press the edges of dough around the filling to make sure they are tight.

4   Preheat oven to 385°F (195°C). In the meantime place the unbaked triangles in the fridge to cool down.

5   Line a baking sheet with parchment paper. Remove triangles from the fridge and place on the parchment paper. Moisten the top of each triangle with some water and sprinkle the coarse sugar on top. Bake the appelflappen for 20 minutes or until golden.

APPELBOLLEN
Dutch apple dumplings

Appelbollen translates as "apple dumplings" and you can easily see why. A whole cored apple is treated to a covering of sugar and cinnamon and the core is stuffed with raisins and nuts. Then the entire apple is sealed in flaky puff pastry to form this delicious treat. This is an easy and perfect last-minute delight to serve to family and friends. Often appelbollen are served with morning coffee. Nothing can beat the heavenly scent of the apples and cinnamon wafting from the oven. These treats really are one of those seasonal specialities that invoke memories of autumn colours, falling leaves and chilly mornings.

🕐 45 MINS　　　🍽 4 CRUNCHY APPELBOLLEN

INGREDIENTS

4 medium apples

4 tbsp golden and red raisins, mixed

1 tbsp walnut small pieces

1 tsp cinnamon

1 ½ tbsp sugar

4 tbsp apple juice or rum

4 puff pastry squares

2 egg yolks

1 tbsp water

INSTRUCTIONS:

1 Preheat the oven to 375°F (190°C). Core the apples but do not peel. In a small bowl, add the raisins, walnuts, cinnamon and 1 tbsp of sugar, and add the apple juice or rum. Mix well and let it soak for a couple of minutes, then fill each apple with the mixture.

2 Place each apple, top down on a square piece of puff pastry and wrap the apple, ensuring all sides are covered and sticking to the apple.

3 Line a baking sheet with parchment paper. Place each apple on the baking sheet, smooth side up. Make an egg mixture with the yolks and the water, and brush onto the dough. Sprinkle all four apples with the remaining sugar. Place in the oven and bake for 20-25 minutes, until golden brown.

ZEEUWSE BOLUS

Dutch cinnamon buns

These Dutch cinnamon rolls of Jewish origin are made by taking white bread dough and coating it in dark brown sugar and cinnamon before being twisted into shape and baked. The resulting sweet pastry is often eaten with coffee. The flat underside can be spread with butter if desired. They are especially delicious when eaten warm. Historically the bolus is said to have been created during the 17th century in Zeeland. Every year since 1998 the Dutch Baking Centre in Zeeland has held a bolus baking championship.

⏱ 1 HOUR 30 MIN

🍽 4 SERVINGS

INGREDIENTS

3 ½ cups flour

1 tbsp active dry yeast

1 ¼ cups milk, warm

½ tsp salt

6 tbsp butter, melted

2 tbsp powdered milk

1 tbsp sugar

For the sugar

2 cups dark brown sugar

1 ½ tsp of cinnamon, ground

INSTRUCTIONS:

1 In a bowl, whisk together the flour, salt, powdered milk and sugar. Dissolve the yeast completely in the warm milk and then add to the dry ingredients. Knead the dough thoroughly for a few minutes, then add the melted butter. Keep kneading for about 15 minutes, then place the dough in a greased bowl. Cover with a damp towel and let rise for 15 minutes in a warm spot.

2 Work the dough carefully and divide into small pieces (around 2 oz/60g each). Roll each piece into a ball. Now mix the brown sugar with the cinnamon and coat each ball with the sugary mix. Place the dough balls back into the bowl, cover and let rise another 15 to 30 minutes. Meanwhile, line a baking sheet with parchment paper.

3 Roll each dough ball out into a rope, about 8 inches (20 cm) long. Cover each rope with more sugar and cinnamon. Hold one end of the rope between your thumb and index finger and then with the other hand roll the dough rope around your index finger. Tuck the end of the rope underneath the roll and place them on the parchment paper. Leave sufficient space between the rolls (1-2 inches/3-5 cm). Sprinkle more sugar on the rolls, cover and let rise for at least an hour or until doubled in size.

4 Preheat the oven to 450°F (230°C). Sprinkle any leftover sugar on the rolls and bake the cinnamon rolls for about 7-8 minutes. Keep an eye on the rolls since the sugar burns quickly. The Zeeuwse bolus will be gooey and sticky, so make sure to let them cool for a bit.

SAUCIJZENBROODJES

Dutch sausage rolls

Buttery puff pastry is stuffed with seasoned mincemeat to form a delicious golden sausage roll. They are best served warm, and can make a nice light lunch when served with a salad. Not surprisingly, saucijzenbroodjes are found in fast food outlets and train stations throughout the Netherlands. These sausage rolls are a favourite quick, on the go Dutch snack. They are a bit messy to eat but are delicious and filling thanks to those layers of flaky, buttery pastry!

🕐 45 MINS   🍽 32 SAVOURY SAUCIJZENBROODJES

INGREDIENTS

1 lb (450g) lean ground beef

4 sheets puff pastry, thawed

1 tsp water

1 egg

2 tbsp milk

2 pinches nutmeg (⅛ tsp)

freshly ground pepper to taste (¼ tsp)

1 egg yolk

1 tsp salt

½ cup bread crumbs

1 tsp Worcestershire sauce

INSTRUCTIONS:

1 Preheat oven to 400°F (200°C). Line a baking sheet with parchment paper.

2 Unfold puff pastry sheets and cut each rectangular sheet in half lengthwise to create 8 separate sheets.

3 In a large mixing bowl combine the ground beef, 1 egg, 2 tbsp milk, 1 tsp salt, 2 pinches nutmeg, freshly ground pepper ½ cup bread crumbs and 1 tsp Worcestershire sauce. Mix thoroughly using your hands.

4 Divide into 8 equal portions and roll each of the beef portions into the shape of a sausage. Place the beef sausage in the middle of a puff pastry sheet (across the length of each sheet). Enclose each beef sausage by folding the pastry sheets and, using wet fingers, pinching the top and bottom edges together. Now cut each pastry into 4 equal rolls, thereby creating a total of 32 saucijzenbroodjes.

5 Beat the egg yolk with water and brush the egg mixture over the rolls.

6 Place the pastry rolls onto the baking sheet and bake for about 20 minutes or until the pastry is crisp and golden.

THE WAFFLE BAKER BY ALEXANDER HUGO BAKKER KORFF (CA. 1850-82)

BAKKER ARENT OOSTWAARD BY JAN HAVICKSZ STEEN (CA. 1625–1679)

BAKED FRUITS

GEBAKKEN PEREN
Dutch baked pears

As the leaves start to change to their autumn colours, the pear season begins and the gebakken peren return to the dinner table! Gebakken peren are baked pears, which make a wonderful autumn and winter dessert. While it's possible to make this dish any time of the year, the seasonality of pears lends this to cooler days. Sticky, sweet syrup is mixed with the fruit and flavoured with warming hints of cinnamon. These baked pears are perfect as a warm dessert for colder nights served with cream, ice cream or even yogurt!

 45 MINS   6 DELICIOUS PEAR HALVES

INGREDIENTS

3 large pears, firm

1 cup sugar, divided

3 tbsp butter

1 cup of water

1 tbsp unseasoned breadcrumbs

1 tbsp vanilla extract

2 tbsp chopped hazelnuts

INSTRUCTIONS:

1   Preheat oven to 350°F (180°C). Cut the pears in half (don't remove the stem or skin). Melt the butter in a skillet and place the pears cut side down. Fry the pears at a low temperature for about 10 minutes until they are golden on the cut sides. Place the pears with the cut side up in an oven dish, sprinkle with a tablespoon of sugar and the breadcrumbs and bake for 20 minutes.

2   While the pears are baking, add the rest of the sugar to the butter in the skillet. Stir carefully and also add the vanilla. Once the sugar is fully absorbed by the butter, add the water. Keep stirring over heat until the sauce thickens and caramelizes, then add the hazelnuts and remove from heat.

3   Take the pears out of the oven, place on a plate and pour the hazelnut caramel sauce over them.

STOOFPEREN
Dutch stewed pears

Once pear season begins, this is another dish that appears on many Dutch tables. Stoofperen are pears poached or stewed in red wine. They make a wonderful part of a meal on colder days, especially in December. With the addition of cinnamon, cloves and lemon peel, the aroma these stewing pears give off is not only wonderful, but also brings a hint of Christmas spice to the kitchen. They can be eaten with roast meats as part of a main meal, or as a dessert with whipped cream, ice cream or yogurt. They taste so good eaten warm, but are also delicious when cold.

🕓 2 HOURS 45 MIN   🍽 4-6 SERVINGS

INGREDIENTS

2 lb (1 kg) small stewing pears

3 cloves

1 piece fresh lemon rind

2 cinnamon sticks

4 tbsp soft brown sugar

1 cup red wine

6 tbsp black currant liqueur

INSTRUCTIONS:

1 Peel the pears and leave whole with stems intact.

2 Stick the cloves into the lemon rind. Put the pears, lemon zest, cinnamon sticks and sugar in a large pan and pour in the red wine and liqueur. Add enough water to just cover the pears.

3 Bring to boil and leave the pears to simmer, covered, for 2 ½ hours until tender.

4 Lift the pears carefully out of the pan, serve on a plate with some cinnamon ice cream and whipped cream.

APPELBEIGNETS
Dutch apple fritters

These lovely little apple treats look a lot like doughnuts thanks to their round shape with a hole in the centre. They are in fact apple slices dipped in batter and fried. They taste best when eaten warm, straight from the pan. They are a brilliant snack, although if not eaten relatively quickly, the batter can go a little soft, so it's better to not make them too far in advance! They are often eaten on New Year's Eve. The word "beignet" has been used in France since the 16th century and referred to deep filled pastries which are fried. It entered the Dutch language sometime in the 18th century.

🕐 45 MINS   🍽 4-6 SERVINGS

INGREDIENTS

1 cup flour

3 large apples, peeled and cored, then sliced thinly into rings

1 ¾ tsp baking powder

3 tbsp sugar

1 tsp ground cinnamon

½ tsp salt

1 cup milk

1 egg

Oil for frying

Cinnamon sugar and powdered sugar for dusting

INSTRUCTIONS:

1   In a small bowl, lightly beat the milk and egg.

2   In a large bowl, mix the flour, baking powder, sugar, cinnamon and salt. Gradually mix the milk/egg mixture into the dry ingredients until the batter is thin enough to dip the apples yet thick enough to stick. Add more flour or milk as needed to reach the necessary consistency. Let the batter set for 15 minutes.

3   Meanwhile, heat the oil in a deep skillet or deep-fryer to 350 °F (180°C).

4   Line a baking sheet with paper towels. Take a couple slices at a time, dip the apple rings into the batter until fully coated, then add to the hot oil. Fry for ca. 4 minutes, until puffy and golden brown, flipping them halfway. Carefully transfer to the paper towels, drain and allow to cool a bit.

5   Sprinkle the appelbeignets generously with cinnamon sugar then a dusting of powdered sugar. Serve warm.

NEW YEAR'S MADNESS

The Dutch celebrate New Year's Eve, aptly called Oud en Nieuw (old and new), in a variety of unique ways. Aside from the notable tradition of everyone and anyone setting off elaborate firework displays across the nation, the Dutch also enjoy some truly delectable delights on the 31st of December.

If on New Year's Day, the doughy treats and boozy beverages from the night (or year) before have you feeling sluggish, you can always head to the seaside with thousands of your compatriots for a frigid dip! Of all the wacky Dutch traditions, I must say, this is definitely one of my favourites. What better way to start the new year than wading into the frigid winter waters of the North Sea alongside thousands of equally crazy Dutchies! The New Year's dive/swim takes place in over 130 locations across the country. The seaside town of Scheveningen gathers the largest crowd, with over 10,000 arctic swimmers usually in attendance. Similar dives are held all over the world. However, the Netherlands boasts the most dive sites and the largest number of scantily-clad participants.

Now back to the food...let's start with the most celebrated of New Year's Eve nibbles: oliebollen! As soon as the temperature drops in the Netherlands, outdoor market stands and stalls start selling these sweet treats on nearly every corner. The smell alone will have your mouth watering before you even take the first bite. Who wouldn't love deep-fried balls of dough covered in powdered sugar?! The direct translation of oliebol is, you guessed it, "oily ball", the Dutch answer to the American doughnut. Due to its substantial nature, it is certainly not something you'd want to eat every week; however, on a cold winter day or evening, nothing quite celebrates the start of the festive season like a fresh warm oliebol!

OLIEBOLLEN
Dutch doughnuts

Oliebollen, or 'oil balls' as they literally translate, are a little bit like doughnuts. The first recipe can be found in the old Dutch cookbook *De Verstandige Kock* from 1667. Incidentally, the first oliebol was not a ball, but a flat cake. Round scoops of batter, often containing raisins, currents or other fruit, are dropped into hot oil and deep fried to create a crunchy snack. They are often served as a traditional snack during Christmas and as a fun treat on New Year's Eve! They can also be found at market stalls or at carnivals and funfairs. Oliebollen are usually served covered in sugar like traditional doughnuts. Definitely a nice, crispy treat freshly hot from the fryer!

🕐 2 HOURS 30 MINS   🍽 4-6 SERVINGS

INGREDIENTS

2 cups flour

1 cup lukewarm milk

1 package dry yeast

2 tsp salt

1 egg, lightly beaten

1 ½ cups raisins

1 apple, peeled, cored and chopped

Oil (for deep frying)

Powdered sugar

INSTRUCTIONS:

1 Add a ¼ cup of the milk to a large cup and stir in the yeast until dissolved.

2 In a large bowl, combine the flour, salt, the remaining milk and the egg. Then add the yeast mixture, raisins and apple and mix thoroughly. Set aside and keep in a warm place until doubled.

3 In a large pot heat oil for frying. To check whether the oil is at the right temperature, stand the handle of a wooden spoon in the oil. If little bubbles form around it, the oil is ready.

4 Using two metal spoons shape balls out of the dough and drop them into the hot oil a few at a time.

5 Deep fry for about 8 minutes (The oliebollen will sink to the bottom of the pan and should then pop right back up). Carefully remove the oliebollen and drain on a paper towel.

6 Immediately sprinkle powdered sugar over the oliebollen and set aside to cool.

MEID MET OLIEBOLLEN BY AELBERT CUYP (CA. 1652)

SINTER KLAAS

SINTERKLAAS

Sinterklaas is arguably the most beloved of all Dutch holidays and traditions — and one that Dutch people are fiercely proud of. The modern-day figure of Santa Claus is actually derived from the Dutch Sinterklaas figure who was named after St. Nicholas, a bishop living in 3rd century Turkey.

The holiday season in the Netherlands officially starts in mid-November, with the arrival of Sinterklaas and his legion of helpers (Zwarte Pieten). Sint arrives by steamboat from Spain, where he is said to live year- round, and parades through town on his white horse to the glee of Dutch children everywhere.

Celebrated on the fifth of December, Sinterklaasavond (Sinterklaas night) or Pakjesavond (present night) is a family affair featuring festive food, treats, gift-giving, and poems.

The celebration of Sinterklaas in the Netherlands has taken place for centuries. Jan Steen, the quintessential Dutch Golden Age painter, captured the festive occasion in his 1665 painting entitled, *Het Sint Nicolaasfeest* (The Feast of Saint Nicholas). This painting is now in Amsterdam's Rijksmuseum and it portrays a Dutch family celebrating Sinterklaas in their family home on the night of December 5th. This centuries-old scene could still easily depict modern day celebrations: a "nice" daughter unpacking toys from a shoe, with a "naughty" older brother in tears at the sight of his empty shoe. A third brother looks on, laughing, as the rest of the family inspect the nearby chimney for traces of Sint's entrance. Most notable, the painting includes a multitude of baked treats: kruidnoten, waffles, duivekater, taaitaai and speculaas, which are all still very much a part of today's Sinterklaas traditions!

From pepernoten, speculaas to chocolate letters, Sinterklaas and the holiday season in the Netherlands abound with uniquely Dutch sweet treats. Don't let their long-standing history scare you off; their recipes are, in fact, a piece of cake!

DUTCH KIDS DRESSED UP AS "PIETEN", SINTERKLAAS' LITTLE HELPERS

KRUIDNOTEN
Mini spiced cookies

Kruidnoten, "spice nuts" are traditionally associated with Sinterklaas who visits on December 5th. These lovely little bite-sized cookies make an excellent Christmas treat. Kruidnoten are small, crunchy, spiced cookies containing exotic spices like cinnamon, ginger, cardamom and cloves. All these spicy flavours are of course associated with the festive season. You can find many varieties of kruidnoten these days, such as dark and white chocolate covered ones. It is said that Sinterklaas' helpers, the Pieten, are crazy for kruidnoten and they always pass out (or throw!) these cookies to children during the annual Sinterklaas parade.

4 HOURS   1 TRAY OF YUMMINESS

INGREDIENTS

1 cup self-rising flour

2 tbsp butter

¾ cup brown sugar

1 egg

½ tsp ginger

1 tsp ground aniseed

2 tsp cinnamon

1 tsp white pepper

1 tsp salt

INSTRUCTIONS:

1 Knead all the ingredients together until you have a nice, stiff dough (add a bit of water if it's too stiff). Wrap the dough and let it rest in the fridge for at least a few hours so that the spices and flavours can blend (ideally leave it overnight).

2 Preheat oven to 400°F (200°C) and line a baking sheet with parchment paper. Take small pieces of dough, roll them into little balls and place them on parchment paper. Flatten them a bit by slightly pressing down.

3 Bake the kruidnoten for about 15 minutes until nicely browned. Let them cool on a rack. But watch out for thieving Pieten who will try to get their hands on them whenever they can!

PEPERNOTEN
Dutch honey & anise cookies

Like kruidnoten, pepernoten are associated with Sinterklaas and once again are little bite-sized cookies. These days many people actually mistakenly refer to kruidnoten as pepernoten, but that is incorrect (as many a Dutchie will point out whenever they can). Pepernoten are a lighter brown colour than kruidnoten and contain spices like anise as well as sugar and traditional rye flour. They have a chewy texture when first made, but harden after a while and become more crunchy. pepernoten are a lovely treat that kids can help make and are a wonderful aromatic addition to your holiday baking list!

🕐 4 HOURS　　🍽 1 TRAY OF YUMMINESS

INGREDIENTS

3 ⅓ cups rye flour

½ cup honey

¼ cup water

½ cup brown sugar (fine)

1 tbsp baking powder (sifted)

½ tsp salt

Vegetable oil (to grease)

1 ½ tbsp ground aniseed

INSTRUCTIONS:

1　Heat the honey with 2 ¾ tablespoons of the water and the sugar until the mixture on medium heat until the sugar is fully dissolved.

2　Add the rye flour and salt to a large bowl. Add the liquid sugar/honey mixture and mix well using a hand mixer with a dough hook attachment. Make sure to knead the dough well.

3　Grease plastic wrap with vegetable oil and cover the dough with the plastic wrap. Allow the dough to rest for one day at room temperature.

4　Once the dough has rested for about 24 hrs, preheat the oven to 340°F (170°C). Now add the remaining 1 ⅓ tbsp of water, the ground anise and baking powder to the dough and knead thoroughly.

5　Rub a bit of the oil onto your hands and roll little balls, about the size of a marble. Place the dough balls into a round cake tin and pack them densely (it's fine if the pepernoten touch each other).

6　Place in the oven and bake the pepernoten for 20 minutes until golden brown. The pepernoten should be a bit chewy and bouncy when pressed.

SPECULAAS
Dutch shortcrust biscuit

Speculaas is a spiced, crunchy cookie usually made for Sinterklaas which is celebrated in the Netherlands on December 5th. They are flat backed, but are traditionally shaped like a Dutch windmill or stamped with images associated with the story of St Nicholas. You can use a speculaas mold or cookie cutters. Once again, these cookies, which don't rise much, are flavoured with spices such as cinnamon, ginger and clove. They are lovely little biscuits for the holiday season and are popular with children and grown ups alike.

🕐 45 MINS   🍽 24 SERVINGS

INGREDIENTS

3 cups flour

1 ½ cups brown sugar

1 cup butter

1 egg

2 tbsp milk

1 tsp baking powder

1 ½ tsp ground cinnamon

¼ tsp salt

½ tsp ground nutmeg

½ tsp ground cloves

½ cup chopped blanched almonds (optional)

INSTRUCTIONS:

1   In a bowl, soften the butter and then gradually add and combine the remaining ingredients. Knead thoroughly until fully mixed.

2   Place the dough in the fridge and let rest for a few hours. This gives the spices and other ingredients more time to properly blend.

3   Divide dough in half. On a lightly floured surface roll one portion of the dough to ⅛ inch (3 mm) thickness.

4   Cut into desired shapes, place on a greased cookie sheet and decorate with almonds (optional). If you want to use traditional wooden moulds then it is important to rub the inside thoroughly with flour (this will make it easier for the cookies to come out afterwards).

5   Repeat with the second half of the dough.

6   Bake in a preheated oven at 350°F (180°C) for 10-15 minutes, or until browned. Remove and allow to cool.

TAAITAAI

Dutch chewy cookies

Taaitaai is another Sinterklaas treat that is popular with both kids and adults! These taaitaai cookies, which translate as "tough tough", look like gingerbread men since they are traditionally made in the shape of a man (Sinterklaas himself), though you can make them in any shape you like. They are very tasty, but hard, chewy and usually eaten as a treat with a hot cocoa drink. The recipe is very similar to pepernoten, as pepernoten were often made from leftover taaitaai dough. While taaitaai may look like gingerbread men, they taste differently as they are not flavoured with ginger but with honey and aniseed.

 45 MINS   🍽 24 SERVINGS

INGREDIENTS

2 cups self-rising flour

2 tbsp pancake syrup

⅓ cup honey

1 egg

½ tsp salt

3 tsp cinnamon

1 tsp ground aniseed

½ tsp nutmeg

½ tsp ground cloves

INSTRUCTIONS:

1. Warm the syrup and honey and mix together.

2. In a large bowl add the flour and mix in all the spices and salt. Then add the syrup/honey mixture and knead thoroughly into a flexible, non-sticky dough (Add small amounts of water if necessary). Wrap the dough in plastic film and place in the fridge for several hours (ideally 24 hrs to let the spices and aromas fully mix).

3. Preheat oven to 350°F (180°C) and line a baking sheet with parchment paper. Dust a work space with flour. Roll out the dough into a thin layer and cut out the shapes. Place the dough pieces onto the baking sheet and brush each one with beaten egg. Bake for about 20-25 minutes and then let cool on a rack.

BANKETSTAAF

Almond paste -filled pastry log

Banketstaaf has a yummy flaky pastry on the outside and is filled inside with almond paste. They are traditionally eaten at Christmas time. They are fantastic with a coffee or a mug of hot tea. Banketstaaf is traditionally made in a long log shape and cut into bite-sized pieces. There is something wonderfully simple about these treats, with their flaky, crumbly pastry and sweet filling. They are fairly quick and easy to make and fun to share with a friend who drops by for a visit.

🕐 40 MINS   🍽 2 LOGS

INGREDIENTS

10.5 oz (300 g) ready-rolled
puff pastry, thawed

1 egg

Almond paste:

1 cup raw blanched almonds

½ cup granulated sugar

1 large egg

1 tsp lemon zest

1 tbsp almond flavoring

INSTRUCTIONS:

1 Preheat the oven to 400°F (205°C).

2 Add the almonds, sugar, almond flavouring and zest to a food processor and grind for a few minutes until very fine. Add the egg and grind more until you have a fine paste. Store in the fridge.

3 Lightly dust a work space with a bit of flour. Unfold the puff pastry and carefully roll the dough out to a 9 x 9 inch square (23 x 23 cm). Cut the dough in half and you will have two 9 x 4.5 inch pieces.

4 Roll the almond paste into two logs that are a bit shorter lengthways than the pastry and place on the pastry. Wet the edges of the pastry slightly and fold in the short ends first and then fold over long sides and press at the seams.

5 Carefully turn the pastry over with the seam at the bottom and brush with the beaten egg. Bake for 25 minutes, or until the pastry turns golden brown. Remove from the oven and set aside to cool.

GEVULDE SPECULAAS
Dutch filled spice cake

Gevulde speculaas is a giant cookie tart, filled with sweet almond paste and flavoured with a magnificent holiday spice mix. The dough is softer than that of a normal cookie mixture thanks to the egg yolk and milk, but it's the spicy, sweet paste filling that makes it so delicious. This is one of those recipes you can make all year around, but has significance for a lot of people around the holidays and during Sinterklaas.

(L) 40 MINS   🍽 6

INGREDIENTS

For the speculaas spices:

1 tsp ground cloves,

½ tsp nutmeg

1 tsp ginger.

1 tsp cardamom

1 tsp coriander

1 tsp of anise

For the baking:

whole almonds without skins for decoration

1 large egg

Almond paste:

1 cup raw blanched almonds

½ cup granulated sugar

1 large egg

1 tsp lemon zest

1 tbsp almond flavoring

For the dough:

1 ½ cups all purpose flour

1 cup brown sugar

¾ cup butter

1 tsp baking powder

Pinch salt

INSTRUCTIONS:

1   Add the almonds, sugar, almond flavouring and zest to a food processor and grind for a few minutes until very fine. Add the egg and grind more until you have a fine paste. Store in the fridge.

2   In a large bowl, add the flour, baking powder, sugar, salt and spices and mix thoroughly. Soften the butter and add it to the dry ingredients. Knead until you get a smooth dough. Add a bit of milk if necessary. Wrap dough in plastic film and put in the fridge for a few hours (the longer you let the dough rest the better the spices will blend with the dough).

3   Preheat oven to 350°F (180°C). Grease a shallow baking pan 8×10 inch (20×26 cm) or, round with a diameter 10 inches (26 cm). Divide the dough into two parts and roll out both portions on a lightly floured surface until they are roughly the size of the baking pan.

4   Place one of the layers in the pan pressing it lightly to ensure it fills the entire pan. Lightly beat the egg with a teaspoon of cold water and brush ⅓ of the egg mix over the dough layer in the pan.

5   Roll out the almond paste until it is the size of the pan. Gently place it over the dough in the pan and press the paste lightly down. Brush the next ⅓ of the egg over it.

6   Place the second layer of dough on top of the paste, press it lightly, and make as smooth as possible. Brush the last ⅓ of the egg over the dough.

7   Decorate the pastry with the almonds. Use traditional patterns or be creative! Put the pan in the oven and bake for 40 minutes. Let cool completely in the pan, then cut it in portions as you like.

CHOCOLADELETTERS

Dutch chocolate letters

Chocolate letters are associated with the festivities around Sinterklaas. Children often receive their initials made in chocolate either on Sinterklaas eve or in their shoe on the days leading up to Sinterklaasavond. The recipe is very simple, so why buy store-bought letters when you can easily make them yourself! Your child will simply be delighted to have the first letter of their name in rich chocolate. If you make your own, you can add decorations that you know each child will like and that will make them even more special!

(L) 2.5 HOURS   8 SMALL LETTERS

INGREDIENTS

1 lb chocolate (450g)

4 oz (120g) butter, room temperature

Requires a pastry bag

INSTRUCTIONS:

1   Melt ¾ of the chocolate over a pot with warm water (or in the microwave). Be very careful not to burn the chocolate. Remove the melted chocolate from the stove and stir in the rest of the chocolate. Whip the butter until fluffy and then stir into the chocolate.

2   Tape parchment paper to a baking sheet. Add your preferred nozzle to a pastry bag and fill the bag with melted chocolate. Now create the chocolate letters on the parchment paper. If you like, you can decorate the letters with sprinkles, kruidnoten and other goodies.

3   Once you have finished, place the letters in a cool area to rest for about 2 hours.

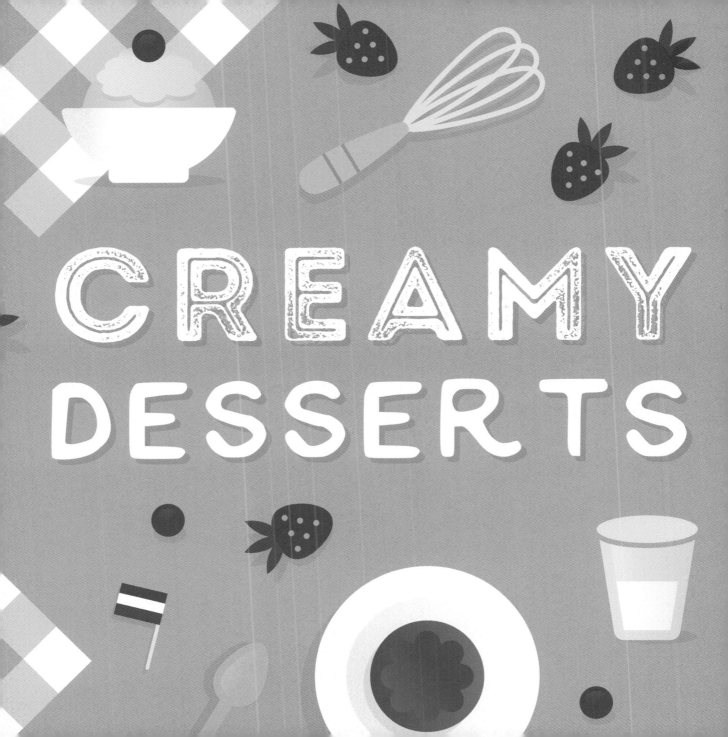

CREAMY
DESSERTS

THE DUTCH AND DAIRY

The Dutch clearly have a long-standing love affair with dairy. Walk into any Dutch home, open the refrigerator, and you are certain to find a bounty of dairy-laden treats. Of course, milk, butter, yogurt and cheese are staples in many homes around the world, but the Dutch differ in the sheer quantity of their consumption. Based on the latest data, the Dutch are the third-highest consumers of dairy in the world — beaten only by their Scandinavian neighbours, Finland and Sweden!

In my native homeland, Canada, we too have many a cow grazing on grassy fields, but drinking milk is a pastime mainly reserved for wee ones. I fondly remember sipping milk from the carton until about the age of eight, but I believe that was the last time I drank a full glass of the white stuff (not even the clever, celeb-laden 'milk mustache' ads of the '90s could convince me). When I came to the Netherlands I gazed in shock, mouth wide open, at the rows and rows of fully-grown Dutchies (women and men) sipping on cartons of milk at lunchtime. Such a sight would rarely be seen outside the Netherlands.

The Netherlands has a long-standing history in the production and consumption of milk, butter and cheese. The dairy industry is one of the largest and most vital agricultural sectors in the Netherlands and responsible for a healthy chunk of the economy. A whopping 27% of the entire country's surface area is grassland and meadow, allowing for over 1.6 million dairy cows to roam — to put that in perspective, that's nearly one cow for every 10 Dutch people. Holy cow!

Dutch dairy is not only popular at home, but also abroad. If you fancy yourself some Gouda or Edam cheese, you are certainly not alone; export revenues for dairy bring in over 7.7 billion euros annually.

It has been said that there is a link between the Dutch's superior stature (i.e. the tallest people in the world) and their copious consumption of dairy. A unique study linked the number of cows per capita to the height of a country's people — and it was no surprise the Dutch, literally, came out on top!

CHOCOLADEVLA

Dutch chocolate custard

Chocoladevla is a smooth, silky chocolate custard. And who doesn't love chocolate! In fact, the word 'vla' originated in the 13th century and refers to a custard-like topping used on cakes and pastries. The Dutch are famous for their chocolate treats and this one is no exception. In addition to the chocolate vla, there are many different flavours of vla, lots of which can be bought in Dutch supermarkets. Chocoladevla is easy to make and is a wonderful dessert all by itself, though you can add whipped cream or even dip fruit slices into it for an additional treat.

🕐 30 MIN   🍽 2-3 SERVINGS

INGREDIENTS

⅓ cup cocoa powder

2 ¼ cups milk

¼ cup cornstarch

⅓ cup sugar

Pinch of salt

INSTRUCTIONS:

1 In a bowl, whisk together the cornstarch, cocoa powder, sugar and salt. Add a cup of milk and whisk thoroughly until the chocolate mixture is smooth and without lumps.

2 In a saucepan, heat the rest of the milk, add the chocolate mixture to the pan and whisk together. After the mixture comes to a boil, keep stirring for about 1-2 minutes until it starts to thicken. Remove from the stove and pour into a bowl. Cover with plastic film and cool in the fridge. Stir before serving.

GRIESMEELPUDDING

Dutch grits pudding

Griesmeelpudding is often considered old fashioned, but it's a lovely comforting, delicious pudding made with wheat grits and topped with a fruity syrup sauce. It is set in a mould which allows you to make fun or unusual shapes. It can be served with poached fruit on the side and makes for a unique dish. Griesmeelpudding will surely invoke some warm feelings and nostalgic memories in many a Dutchie who will remember eating it as a child at their oma's house.

🕒 30 MIN   🍽 1 WIGGLY GRIESMEELPUDDING

INGREDIENTS

4 cups milk

1 cup grits

¾ cup sugar

1 slice lemon peel

1 tsp vanilla essence

INSTRUCTIONS:

1   In a saucepan, bring the milk to a boil, then add the lemon peel and sugar and whisk until the sugar has completely dissolved. Mix in the grits and bring everything back to a boil. Make sure to keep stirring well to avoid burning. Turn the heat down and cook everything for about 6-7 minutes. Mix in the vanilla. Make sure to stir regularly.

2   Hold the pudding form under cold water. Remove the lemon peel and then pour the rest of the pudding into the form. Place the form in the fridge to cool. It may take 5-6 hours for the pudding to set.

3   Pour warm water over the outside of the pudding form, gently loosen the sides, turn the pudding form upside down onto a plate and gently lift the form.

TIP
Serve with a berry or cherry sauce on top and on the sides

HEMELSE MODDER
Dutch chocolate mousse

The Dutch have played a very important role in creating what we know now as chocolate! At one point in time Dutch merchants controlled almost the whole cocoa bean trade! So it's little wonder that yummy chocolate recipes like Hemelse Modder are a Dutch tradition. Translated as "heavenly mud", Hemelse Modder is a creamy, thick chocolate mousse which makes for a heavenly indulgent treat. You can top it with cream or if you prefer add a pinch of cinnamon for a bit of a twist.

⏲ 2 HOURS   🍽 4 SERVINGS

INGREDIENTS

2 cups heavy whipping cream

8 oz (225g) semi-sweet or dark chocolate

2-3 tbsp sugar

INSTRUCTIONS:

1 Add half of the whipping cream and all of the chocolate to a saucepan. Stir well on medium heat until the chocolate is just melted. Remove from the stove and let it cool down.

2 Whip the rest of the whipping cream with the sugar until stiff. Gently fold the cold chocolate mixture into the whipping cream. Carefully pour the mousse into serving dishes and cover each one with plastic film. Place the dishes in the fridge and let mousse set for about 1-2 hours.

TIP
Serve with whipped cream or fresh fruit. Delicious!

DUTCH LICORICE: DROP

There is no denying that Dutch people love licorice. They, in fact, eat the most amount of licorice per capita of any people in the world. This is however, not the kind of North American licorice (red or slightly salty black) you may be used to; the Dutch prefer a much stronger variety that many foreigners find, well... inedible.

Dutch drop comes in a variety of different flavours and sorts. There are four primary types of drop: soft & sweet, soft & salty, hard & sweet and hard & salty. Drop can be bought just about anywhere in the Netherlands, but can also be found in drugstores and pharmacies as the Dutch believe it has medicinal properties (mainly concerning sore throats and tummy aches). When I suffered from low blood pressure during my pregnancies, my very lovely and capable Dutch midwife prescribed...you guessed it...drop. I was dumbfounded, but it appeared to do the trick!

The different versions of drop can seem endless, everything from Engelse drop (English) to honingdrop (honey), muntdrop (mint) to the obscure oceaandrop (ocean –huh?). Drop doesn't come in spiraly tubes like it does across the pond, but rather pedestrian shapes such as circles, squares, diamonds, ovals, cubes and coins. I've recently spotted a trend on the supermarket shelves... themed shaped drop: licorice cars, anyone? Indeed, try autodrop! Cat lover? Well, then you're sure to love Katjesdrop! Of course the pinnacle of strong-tasting Dutch licorice is quite scary: Dubbel Zout. Try it at your peril!

FUN FACT:

The Dutch consume the most licorice in the world. How much do you ask? Roughly more than 4 pounds of it a year, per person!

While surfing the internet, I recently came across a disturbing trend: Dutch people feeding drop to non-Dutch people and recording it. Check YouTube for some laughs and remember...the next time a smiling Dutch person offers you "a candy", proceed with caution!

DROP
Dutch salty licorice

"Drop" is the Dutch word for licorice. It does have some licorice in it along with salt and ammonium chloride. However it is not for the faint of heart. The Dutch love their sweets, including drop. It has a salty, ammonia taste that makes drop less palatable to those who haven't grown up with it. So it's very unlikely you'll have non-Dutch compatriots clamoring for this recipe! That being said, drop is exceptionally popular in the Netherlands and homemade drop is always nicer than store-bought. Therefore, if you're tempted to try making it or love the stuff already, then this is the recipe for you!

L 30 MINS   4 SERVINGS

INGREDIENTS

1 cup water

5.5 oz (150 g) licorice root

3 tsp brown sugar

½ tsp salmiak

2 sheets gelatin

3 tsp flour

INSTRUCTIONS:

1 Cut the licorice root into small pieces of about half an inch (1 cm) in size. Bring the water to a boil and add the licorice root to it.

2 Let the licorice root boil for about 5 minutes, then pour everything through a sieve and collect the licorice water in clean small saucepan. Place the saucepan with licorice water back on the stove. Leave to simmer until there is only about one fifth of your water left. Then lower the heat.

3 Stir the brown sugar into the water and wait for it to dissolve. Then add the salmiak.

4 Soak a sheet of gelatin in a bowl of water for about 5 minutes.

5 In the meantime, make a paste of the 3 tsp of flour and a small dash of water.

6 While stirring, add the soaked gelatin and the flour paste to the licorice water. Make sure to stir well to prevent lumps from forming.

7 Keep stirring until you get a smooth and bound mixture. Pour the mixture greased aluminum foil.

8 Let the licorice stand for a few days until it has hardened.

ABOUT US

About the Author

Colleen Geske is the author of the hugely popular blog '*Stuff Dutch People Like*'. She is originally from Winnipeg, Canada and has lived in Europe since 2004. When not busy writing, Colleen spends her days as a senior advisor in international policy. Colleen holds degrees in International Business and Marketing from the University of Manitoba. She currently lives in Amsterdam with her family.

About Stuff Dutch People Like

Stuff Dutch People Like is a celebration of the Netherlands and Dutch culture. It started life as a blog in 2010 and quickly developed a loyal following in the Netherlands and abroad. SDPL now has over 500,000 fans across its various social media platforms and over a quarter of a million regular monthly readers of the blog. The first book under the same title became an instant international bestseller and other books followed as part of the *Stuff Dutch People Like seriess*, including *Stuff Dutch People Say*, *Stuff Dutch People Eat* and *Stuff Dutch Moms Like*. SDPL has also ventured into new product areas and now has an attractive line-up of non-book interior design and lifestyle products. Check out our website to learn more! Tot ziens!
www.stuffdutchpeoplelike.com

OUR BESTSELLING BOOKS

STUFF DUTCH PEOPLE LIKE (THE ORIGINAL)

Blunt, provocative and wickedly funny, *Stuff Dutch People Like* is a satirical look at Dutch culture as seen through the eyes of an outsider. From *Appelmoes* to *Zwarte Piet* and everything in between, *Stuff Dutch People Like* covers it all – and then some!

STUFF DUTCH PEOPLE EAT

From the bestselling *Stuff Dutch People Like* comes this comprehensive celebration of Dutch cuisine. Whether you're looking for festive sweets, traditional tastes or colonial classics, we've got something for every appetite! From breakfast straight through to dessert, *Stuff Dutch People Eat* will lead you through a culinary adventure spanning flavours - and centuries! Discover 40 easy-to-make recipes that are sure to restore your faith in the delightfully delicious Dutch kitchen! *Eet smakelijk!*

YOU KNOW YOU'RE DUTCH, WHEN...

Introducing the ultimate humorous guide to what really makes Dutch people so very...Dutch. This hilarious bestseller will have you nodding your head in agreement -and might just have you wiping away tears of laughter!

OUR BESTSELLING BOOKS

STUFF DUTCH PEOPLE SAY

The hilarious companion to the original *Stuff Dutch People Like* bestseller. *Stuff Dutch People Say* delves deep into the linguistic world of the Lowlands, exploring what happens when Dutch and English collide. From funny Dutch words, incomprehensible Dutch expressions and hysterical examples of Dunglish, we've got you covered!

STUFF DUTCH MOMS LIKE

Stuff Dutch Moms Like investigates why Dutch moms are amongst the happiest in the world-and how they manage to have it all! Filled with hilarious anecdotes, tips and tricks, *Stuff Dutch Moms Like* takes an inside look at parenting in the Netherlands and the secrets to raising the happiest children in the world!

GREETINGS FROM AMSTERDAM

Greetings from Amsterdam is a visual guided tour that takes the reader through the Netherlands' capital city and beyond. Explore Amsterdam's rich history and culture, tour its diverse neighbourhoods, and discover the many colourful festivities that make Amsterdam the dynamic, cosmopolitan city it is today.

OUR PRODUCTS

DUTCH JEWELLERY

STROOPWAFEL TEETHER   BIRTHDAY CALENDAR   DUTCH CHEESE BOARD   TEGELTJES

DUTCH CLOCK

CREDITS